What If You Didn't Have Running Water?

by Miss Gratton's class
with Tony Stead

capstone

Introduction

by May

People have made settlements during different times in history. People traveled to different places and built villages and towns there. They also made sure they had what they needed.

Every settlement needs food, water, shelter, a cozy place to sit, and somewhere to see family and play. The most important things to have in a settlement are food, water, and shelter because they help people survive. The other things are for having fun and playing around.

We have looked at settlements in history, in times when there were no videos, no computer games, and you couldn't go to the café for a snack! We had lots of questions before we researched settlements. What would it be like to have no water taps in the Stone Age? What sort of clothes did the Ancient Egyptians wear? What did the Colonial Americans eat as everyday food? How did people live together, and how was it different from or the same as today? We will be answering a lot of those questions in this book.

Different Settlements

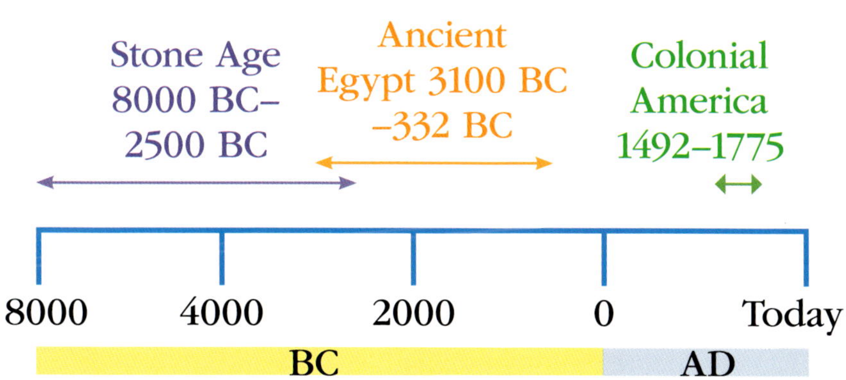

Living in the Stone Age

by Danai, Eva, and Eve

What was living in the Stone Age like? Have you ever wondered what people ate and wore or how they got their food? Living in the Stone Age was very different from living in the world today!

Stone Age Homes

Did you know that early humans lived in caves? They lived in groups and made cave villages. They also made their caves look nice. They decorated the stone walls with paint. Their paintbrushes were just sticks or animal hairs. Sometimes they would use feathers or hollow bones. They used their paints to make pictures of people and animals and do handprints on the walls.

Later, Stone Age people started to build houses out of wood or stone. Stone Age houses were probably rectangular with a cone-shaped roof that was made with things such as grasses, driftwood, or seaweed.

Stone Age Paint Recipe

1 Take colored minerals.
2. Crush them with a rock.
3. Put the minerals on a damp surface, like a rock.
4. Mix the crushed powder with oil or wax if you want. This will make the paint more sticky.
5. Keep your colors in hollow bone tubes.

use this	get this paint color
crushed rocks, clays, and earth	brown, yellows, reds, oranges
charcoal	black
chalk (or crushed bones)	white

Skara Brae Homes

Skara Brae is in Scotland, United Kingdom. People have found ruins of Stone Age houses there. When the archeologists dug up the grass and sand, they discovered houses from the past. We can tell a lot about Stone Age homes from Skara Brae.

The walls of Stone Age houses were very solid. There was not much wood in Skara Brae, so the furniture, such as dressers or tables, were made from stone. The hard stone beds were actually quite comfortable. They had straw mattresses and sheepskin blankets.

In the middle of these houses was a pit that Stone Age people used to cook on and keep warm. All of the family members would gather around the fire and eat what they could find for meals. They did have a place where they prepared the food. It was a pile of neat, stacked rocks with a flat piece of slate on top.

In the early Stone Age, people started making rocks into tools like hand axes or hammers. These tools were made out of flint. Stone tools were used to cut fish or meat, scrape animal skins, or dig up roots to eat.

Getting Food

It is easy to get food today, but what about in the Stone Age times? The Stone Age people lived as hunter-gatherers. This means that instead of growing their food, they hunted for it or they picked nuts and fruit. They traveled from place to place in search of the best hunting grounds. They lived in temporary shelters while hunting. Eventually they learned to grow their own crops and began to settle in one place. These people were the first farmers.

Food We Eat vs. Food in the Stone Age

People Today	People During the Stone Age
We eat eggs from chickens.	The Stone Age humans ate eggs.
We eat fruit and nuts.	The early humans also ate fruit and nuts.
We eat fish.	The Stone Age humans ate fish.
We can have chocolate, sweets, soup, bread, and all sorts of ingredients to make lots of yummy stuff.	The Stone Age humans probably did not mix food, so they did not have these foods.

Food Eaten During the Stone Age

Hunting for Protein

Gigantic animals were alive during the Stone Age. Humans hunted some of these huge animals, like mammoths, for food. Hunters probably tried to kill young, sick, or lonely animals that had become trapped or stuck in muddy swamps. After hunting their prey, the hunters waited until it collapsed, then moved in for the KILL!

We are luckier than the Stone Age humans from long ago! It is much easier to get food today.

Did You Know?

Catching animals would be difficult during the Stone Age. People only had weapons made from wood, stone, and bone, such as wooden spears, stone axes, and bone knives!

What People Wore

Stone Age weather could be very cold, which made clothing essential. A long, long time ago, humans washed and pressed animal skins so they could use them for clothes to keep them warm. In the Stone Age, people would cover their faces and bodies with bright paints made from dyes and pigments. Later, Stone Age people started to string shells together to make some very pretty jewelry.

Dangers in the Stone Age

There were plenty of dangers people were faced with during the Stone Age. People often lived together for protection. For example, the animals were very dangerous. There were saber-toothed tigers, giant bears, and other frightening animals. Another problem was life span. Diseases weren't a big problem, but people had shorter lives. It was very cold, so many people died from the cold.

They all needed to live in a safe place so animals were less likely to come near and so they could stay warm. To be extra sure they were safe, they lit a fire in the entrance of their homes (if they were caves) so all of the animals would not come near. The early humans developed tools to defend themselves from animals or enemies.

Conclusion

Life was very different in the Stone Age. But people lived with their families in groups. Because life was hard, people had to work together to gather the items that they needed.

Life in Ancient Egypt

By Annabelle, Jessica, Lily, and Wills

In Ancient Egypt, people settled by the Nile River. They built towns and cities there. Why did they settle near the Nile River? It was a good for farming and had lots of fruit trees. But what was life like for the Ancient Egyptians? They lived long ago, but in some ways their lives were similar to the way we live today.

Farming

The Ancient Egyptians were good farmers because of the Nile River. The river overflowed each year, covering the ground with a thick layer of silt or mud. This helped fertilize the land and made the land good to farm.

Do you want to know what Ancient Egyptians ate? They ate a lot of bread, and that made wheat the most important crop. The Ancient Egyptians also ate beans, lettuce, onions, figs, dates, grapes, and melons.

Did You Know?

Some farmers trained monkeys to help them during the harvesttime. The monkeys climbed up the trees to collect the fruit.

Egyptian gardens sometimes had flowers and fruit trees around ponds.

Houses

In ancient Egypt, peopled lived in the desert, so there were no forests filled with trees from which to build houses. In order to build houses, the Egyptians made bricks out of mud and straw and left them in the sun to dry. Rich people had stone houses with beds. The poor didn't have much furniture. They just sat on the floor or used low stools. They also slept on straw mats. The poor had only one room and kept their goats and chickens in their courtyard.

Rich Egyptians had comfortable country houses, which had vegetable and flower patches and stables for donkeys and other animals. Servants helped rich people live comfortably. They had to clean, cook, work on the farm, and help around the house.

Settlements grew fast in Ancient Egypt because the farming was good and the houses were easy to build.

Getting Sick in Ancient Egypt

Getting ill in Ancient Egypt could be very dangerous. People didn't have the same medicines as we do today. And they started living closer together, so illness could spread easily. There was no modern medicine. Can you imagine that? If you got sick, there was no modern medicine, like pills, to cure it.

People got sick from the land around the Nile River and the desert lands. One way of getting ill in ancient Egypt was if fine sand got into a person's body. It could get into the person's lungs, and the person could get sick and stop breathing.

Egyptian doctors tried to make medicine carefully, but they didn't understand every illness. Many believed that evil spirits got inside people's bodies or sent poison to their bodies and made them sick. This wasn't true, but they thought it was. Doctors would make the person take medicine that tasted bad to get the evil spirit to leave. So quite a lot of their medicines didn't work. I wouldn't like to get ill in ancient Egypt!

Quiz

Now that you've read about ancient Egypt, try to take this quiz. Put these words in the correct categories:

computers, tablets, paper, fireplaces, medicine, wheat, salt, paint, mummies, pyramids

Now	Ancient Egypt	Both

Find the answer key on page 21.

Children in Ancient Egypt

Most Egyptian parents had quite a few children; however, not all children survived. Their parents took good care of them, but doctors didn't know everything they know today. Lots of children died during birth or of illness.

The education of children from rich homes was very different from poor children. Mostly, only rich boys went to school. In contrast, the poor stayed home. Children learned most things at home. If their parents could read and write, they taught their children. The girls stayed at home and helped their mothers with the cooking and cleaning. They also helped take care of younger siblings and other important things. Only rich girls learned to read and write.

Children's Toys

Many toys were the same as modern ones. Toys included:

- dolls
- balls
- miniature swords and chariots
- animals made out of wood or clay such as dogs, cats, and donkeys
- board games
- spinning tops

What Did Ancient Egyptian Children Wear?

Egypt is a hot country, so people wore light clothes that kept them cool. We can see what they wore from the paintings and sculptures they left. Egyptian clothes covered most of their bodies and were made of plant fibers. Children wore clothes to protect them from the heat. Girls and women wore straight dresses with or without shoulder straps. Men wore square-shaped kilts down to their knees. It was interesting that men and women both wore black eye makeup. This helped protect their eyes from the sun and also helped them look good!

Conclusion

We found out about farming, homes, medicine, and children in Ancient Egypt. We also found out that some things are a lot like today. But people have learned more since ancient times and some things, such as medicine, have gotten better.

Quiz Answer Key

Now: **computers, tablets**
Ancient Egypt: **mummies, pyramids**
Both: **paper, fireplaces, medicine, wheat, salt, paint**,

Settling in America

By Chloe, Eve, and May

More than 400 years ago, people traveled from England to America. They wanted to build a new life there. Some people wanted to worship however they liked. Some people wanted to have lots of land. So they traveled to America by ship, and they had to build everything new. At first, there were no houses, shops, schools, or anything there. The people had to build them all and start again.

Houses in Colonial America

The houses built by the first English settlers had only one room. Many of the houses were built from logs. Others were made with wattle and daub.

What is wattle and daub? The wooden frames of the houses were woven with sticks (wattle). The gaps were filled in with sticky daub. Daub is a mixture of clay, mud, and grass. This makes a sticky mixture that was good for filling in the gaps of the sticks that held up the houses. Then it would dry and become hard. This mixture could also fill in the cracks between logs in log cabins.

How to Make a Log Cabin

The first people to arrive in America had to build their own houses. There were no houses already there for them. They mainly built log cabins. This is how:

Step one

One of the first things the pioneers had to do to build a log cabin was to clear anything that was growing there, such as trees. They would use these trees to build the log cabin.

Step two

They would stack the logs by making notches so that the house stood firmly in position. If only one man was building a log cabin, it would be about 6 or 7 feet tall, but with more help, it would be a bigger and better house to live in.

Step three

To make it feel like home, they would add a bed, a small table, a couple of chairs, and some candles for light.

Swedish pioneers built a log cabin in Pennsylvania around 1650. People can still visit it today.

Food in Colonial America

People brought their cattle, sheep, pigs, and chickens on ships to America from England. But people had to learn how to grow food in the new country. Native Americans helped them learn. Would you want to live in Colonial America? Perhaps this menu will help you decide.

A Colonial American Daily Menu

Breakfast
Breakfast is a bowl of porridge made out of cornmeal (with some syrup) or some bread.

Lunch
On offer today is a choice of meat—lamb, pork, or steak—that is served with bread and vegetables.

Dinner
Dinner today is a meat stew. Maybe you feel like having a meat pie! That will be served with some cider as a treat.

Clothes in Colonial America

Many of the Colonial Americans were Puritans. Many people in England wore velvets and silks, but the Puritans wanted to dress more simply. Their clothing was heavy and sometimes made out of wool or leather. Women often made their own clothes. They spun wool and sewed dresses.

Did You Know?

Puritans were people who wore simple clothes. They didn't want to be fancy. Puritans were very religious and wanted a simpler way of life. That's why they went to America.

What Did Men Wear?

From the top to the bottom, Puritan men wore big hats and long shirts. Over the shirts they wore leather jackets, and sometimes they wore sleeveless leather jackets. They wore breeches, which were baggy trousers that went to their knees. They also wore long wool socks that reached their knees and big leather shoes.

What Did Women Wear?

Puritan women wore caps to cover their hair because it was not supposed to be seen. They also wore long dresses. Under their dresses they wore undershirts. Over the dresses they sometimes wore aprons. On their feet they wore long stockings and plain leather shoes.

In Colonial times women never wore trousers. These days, clothes are warmer, but I like the look of clothes from the older days. But I wouldn't like to wear dresses all the time because it's a bit annoying. They get in the way. And they sometimes caught fire on the kitchen fires in the old days.

People living in different times and in different places wear different clothes from us today. Their clothes suit their time and their place.

Conclusion

No matter the reason people traveled from Europe to America, they all built new lives there and had to work hard. They built log cabins to live in. They farmed and raised animals for food. They usually made their own clothes. But they started over in a new land and developed a new country.

Final Thoughts

by Wills

Now you have learned what daily life was like for people long ago. You learned about the foods people ate, what types of houses they lived in, and what types of clothes they wore. Some of it seems strange to us, but we also learned that some things are still the same today. People still live in groups called families and people still work hard and provide for their families.

Long ago, people may not have had running water, but they were able to manage without that technology to survive. Now that you've learned about life from long ago, would you have wanted to live back then? Could you live without running water?